This Book Belongs To

ISBN: 978-1-7377759-2-8

Oh, No... Hacked Again!

A Story About Online Safety

Written by: Zinet Kemal

Illustrated by: Sasha Izmaylova

Designed & Formatted by: Mia Hay

Edited by: Naomi Books, LLC.

Dedications

I dedicate this book to all children from different walks of life.

Remember that your future is bright and limitless.

Dream big.

You can be anything you want to be!

Acknowledgments

Thank you to my beloved husband, Aman H., who is always my rock, supporting me with all my dreams.

I also thank my four adventurous and kind children, Imran, Elham, Iman and Haroon, who continue to be my everyday inspiration and my reasons for writing this story.

And a huge thank you to my dearest father, Abdella M., and my fierce mother, Murayo O., for their love and unwavering support throughout my lifetime.

A Special Note From The Author

I wrote this book, inspired by the experiences of my own children. It is their story, and if it happened to them, it's likely that it has happened to other families as well.

In this era of the digital world, when kids are spending more time online than ever, everyone needs to be careful. As an individual who works in the cybersecurity field, and most importantly as a mother, I care so much about not only protecting my own children but also children everywhere. I want them all to stay safe online, whether gaming or surfing the internet. That is why I wrote this book for children and their families.

"Oh, No... Hacked Again!" A Story About Online Safety can be an excellent conversation starter about the importance of staying safe online. I also hope it will spark children's interest in the possibility of pursuing a career in the field of cybersecurity when they grow up.

Table of Contents:

Chapter One

The Story Begins

Hey, my name is Elham.

I am eight years old. My two siblings and I love to play games online, especially games on Zokanda, one of the best gaming platforms. Our favorites so far are Qorky and Hibbo.

I also play Kubba because my big brother, Imran, is a pro in that game! My little sister, Iman, and I like to play with him. I know a lot of our school friends, cousins and neighbor kids who play different games on Zokanda.

Did I mention I have been playing Zokanda games my entire life? Okay, okay, I am being a little dramatic. Not my whole life, but since I was four years old.

My parents let us play online games, but they don't like it when we play too much. They are happier when we play outdoors or read books.

They don't want us to play more than two hours a day, but that rarely happens, and we always end up playing longer than that. Why? Because the games are sooo good! Since the beginning of the pandemic lockdown, I know for sure we've played more because we stayed at home more.

Of course, we also like reading books and playing with our adorable little brother, Haroon. But when he naps, we enjoy playing online games, whispering and quietly giggling.

Chapter Two

The Panic

It was a beautiful Tuesday summer morning in Blaine, Minnesota. My siblings and I had just gotten home from playing backyard soccer. The heat from the sun was already making us too exhausted to keep playing.

Both Mom and Dad were working from home on their computers. Haroon was taking his mid-morning nap. It was the perfect time to have some fun, just as planned.

I grabbed my tablet and went straight to Imran's bedroom, ready to start the game. We were all excited because we had been talking about playing together in this huge tournament for over a week. I noticed I was logged out of my account. I thought that was weird, and I tried entering my password, but it didn't work.

A few minutes later...

"Hey, guys, I couldn't log in." Feeling frantic, I almost screamed at my siblings, "I know I put in my password correctly, and I tried three times already!"

"Try again," said Imran, absently, keeping his eyes glued to his screen.

"No, I already tried it again. It doesn't work!" I was freaking out!

"Are you sure? Can you type slowly this time and try again?" Imran suggested.

"Oh, wait," I froze. My mind immediately rushed to the night before.

I was looking to replace my current online avatar and needed free Coin, a digital currency to shop for skins and items on Zokanda. So, I searched for free Coin, and it prompted me to enter my username and password. Then I had to complete some survey and obstacle challenges.

Now, it finally dawned on me.

"Oh, no!" I gasped. " I think I've been hacked! And I think I know what happened."
So, I told Imran and Iman about my adventure from the night before when I was trying to get free Coin. How could I be so naïve? I felt myself begin to panic.

"Imran," I said nervously, "I know you warned me about those surveys and being careful with my password. I don't even know why I thought it was a good idea to enter my username and password. It looked so legit, though."

"This can't be happening again," I moaned.

Yes, you read that right… again!

Chapter Three

The Take Over

A few months ago, one of my online "friends" offered to send Coin to my account. She asked me for my password so she could transfer it. I knew I wasn't supposed to share my password with anyone, but I trusted her. She promised she only needed my password to transfer the Coin. The next thing I knew, I couldn't log back in, and I lost my account. I was devastated.

My mom had already warned us not to share our passwords or any personal information with any of our online friends. She always reminded us not to play online with strangers, but only with people we know from school or in person. She was very serious about it and kept telling us to be cautious and stay safe online.

But, I wasn't.

Now, how would I tell my mom that I got hacked again? I felt awful.

"Why do people scam and trick other people? Why is this always happening to me?" I asked myself out loud. I was sad and felt embarrassed too. I decided not to tell my parents.

"Hey, guys. Mom can't know about this," I warned my siblings. "Okay?"

"Sure, we won't tell her if you don't want us to, but when are we going to play together?" asked Iman, frustrated.

"I don't feel like playing now. You guys go ahead without me. It's my fault, and I should have known better," I told them.

I put my tablet away and went to my bedroom. We had been planning for this game since last week. Why now? Why do I keep falling for such tricks? Lying on my bed, I hugged my pillow and started to cry.

"Elham, please don't be so hard on yourself," Imran said. "It happens to everyone at least once." He and Iman were by my bedside. Apparently, they had followed me to my room.

"It happened to me before, and you both knew about it," said Imran patting my shoulder, trying to calm me down.

"It even happens to adults," he reminded us. "Mom told me grown-ups fall for these tricks, click bad links and enter their passwords into wrong places all the time."

"Oh! I remember what those are called," Iman jumped in. "I heard Mom say they're phishing links. Fishing with 'ph,' not 'f.' Get it?"

My brother and I looked at her and said nothing. She continued, "Guys, you know I'm always careful. I've never lost my account and I've never gotten hacked before either."

"Well, thanks, Smarty-Pants! That makes me feel so much better," I replied sarcastically, rolling my eyes. I buried my face into my pillow.

Imran was right, though. Someone tricked him in the past and lured him into giving his password too. I remembered how upset he was when he lost his account. Also, another time, some kid even threatened Imran, saying he knew his IP address and would leak it unless he showed his face on a chat!

Imran had played with him for almost a year, but he wasn't comfortable showing his face, so he refused. I remember this kid calling himself Imran's "big brother." He told Imran not to talk about him to any member of his family. That terrified Imran. He thought this kid would hack our Wi-Fi and the whole family would be in danger.

Since Imran didn't want to get in trouble, he told me and Iman not to tell our parents.

I was scared, too, but somebody needed to do the right thing. So, I told Mom anyway. She always encouraged us to go to her or Dad if there was a problem, no matter what happened.

That's when Mom blocked the person and told all of us not to trust anyone online or share our personal information. I'm so glad I told her, because I saw how relieved Imran was afterward. Seeing that kid get busted was so awesome!

Chapter Four

Doing The Right Thing

Trying to pick myself up, I asked my siblings, "It's not like I am the only one falling for this, right?"

"Right!" They both answered at the same time. Iman added, "Just go to Mom and remind her about what she told us. You know, about not keeping anything from her or Dad."

"Okay, fine." I gave in. "You're right; Mom did say that." Right then, I decided to do the right thing.

"I will tell her when she finishes her meeting," I announced, still feeling awful.

"Yes! We can probably make it in time for the game," Iman said excitedly.

So, as soon as Mom finished her video call from work, I told her everything.

She listened quietly. I waited anxiously for her response, biting my lip and chewing at my fingernails. She said nothing.

"Is she mad at me?" I thought to myself.

Mom locked off her work computer screen and took a sip from her coffee mug. She then swivelled her chair and looked toward me again, staying silent.
My mind was racing! Why wasn't she saying anything? Oh no, she must be very upset with me. Why wouldn't she be? She would probably ground all of us. I knew it! I should have kept it to myself. I am so doomed!

A few moments later, Mom said, "I am glad you told me."

I exhaled.

"But..." she continued. Then she paused for a minute, which seemed like an hour to me.

Uh, oh. There is a "but," and nothing good ever comes after a "but." Well, usually. I was even more nervous now.

"Entering your password to some random site? Looking for free stuff?" Mom asked, not really expecting an answer. "I mean, given what happened last time and how we talked about not sharing your password, what were you thinking?"

"I know, Mom. But this looked so legit, and I thought the link was from Zokanda itself."

"You have to remember to be more careful. Ask me or Dad to check to see if it's safe before you enter your information or click a suspicious link," she scolded me.

Mom left her home office. I followed her.

"Mom, I lost everything, and there was lots of cool stuff on my account. I can never recover it or have a cool avatar like I had before." Thinking of all the time and effort I had put into my account, my eyes started tearing up, of course.

Mom stopped and hugged me.

"I know it's hard, and I understand," she said. "But think of it this way, you learned another important lesson."

"Last time when you lost your account, you learned to never share your password with anyone," she said. "You can't share it with your close friends either, even if they say, 'I swear' or offer to transfer free Coin, right?" Mom prompted.

"Right," I responded, still feeling foolish.

"But, Mom, she was my friend! She said she would just add Coin to my account. She swore on it four times and literally said she wouldn't hack me."

Now that I think about it, I felt so silly for trusting that girl.

Mom smiled, as if she knew what was going through my mind.

"Now, will you be more cautious about clicking links or giving out your username or password?"

I nodded my head and smiled back at Mom.

Chapter Five

The Lesson

Did I mention my mom is so dope and has the coolest job? Yeah, she is a cybersecurity engineer, who keeps computers safe from bad hackers and bad guys. Like a ninja and a superhero! I want to do that, too, when I grow up... become a cyber hero! Anyway, back to my crisis.

"I promise I will be more careful next time, Mom," I said. "I'm just sad that I lost all my Coin, my account and all my friends."

Mom looked at me. "How about we have lunch first?" She asked. "Then, I need some help with something. It will be a chore for you, so you can earn an allowance to buy your own Coin."

She winked at me with a grin on her face.

My eyes lit up! I jumped up and hugged her. "Thank you, Mom! You are the best!"

Mom squeezed me back. "You are so welcome, Sweetie! I am so glad that you came to me. That was the right thing to do; I'm so proud of you."

"When you create your new account, please don't forget to add two-step verification this time," added my nerdy big brother, sneaking up behind us. "It helps to protect your account one step further."

"Wait, a what step verification, now?" I looked up at him, very confused.

"I can explain and show you how to set it up. I just use my email to do that," said Imran.

"Look at you!" Mom gushed happily. "I knew nothing about computers when I was your age or even much older. You're all so smart!"

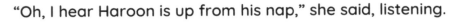

"Oh, I hear Haroon is up from his nap," she said, listening.

"I got him," said Dad, coming down the stairs, holding Haroon in his arms.

I ran upstairs, eager to plan my online shopping spree for some more cool stuff. I couldn't wait to earn my allowance and buy my own Coin. I would get an awesome new avatar!

Although I was still a little sad about losing my account, I am glad I shared everything with my mom. I was happy that my siblings and Mom stood by to support me when I was frustrated. Now that Imran will teach Iman and me about two-step verification and show us how to set it up, my account will be more protected.

Basically, what it means is that we would just need another special code from our email to log into our games, on top of our passwords. I would definitely have to be more careful, never share my password or click any bad links.

I am so lucky. This could have been much worse! I want to protect other kids and teach people about how to keep their information and computers safe from bad guys. You know, just like Mom and other cybersecurity experts do. Plus, I'm going to be an artist too! Painting is my favorite thing to do and I'm good at it. My parents always say I can be anything I want to be.

That afternoon, I had a wonderful time playing with my siblings, including baby Haroon. Everything worked out just fine.

Lessons From The Book

- Never, <u>EVER</u> share your password with anyone. <u>Ever!</u>

- Always listen to your parents about online safety advice and remember to share with them if you run into any online problems.

- Practice online safety by not sharing any personal information online, such as your date of birth, school name, etc.

- Avoid clicking untrusted links and always ask an adult before entering your username and password onto any website or gaming platform.

- Limit your screen time by aiming to play outdoors, do indoor activities or read more books.

- Remember, cybersecurity is a great career option to consider. Children can learn about it now and prepare themselves by practicing online safety.

Did You Know The Meaning of These Words?

- <u>Cybersecurity</u> - The practice of protecting devices, networks, systems and data through controls, technologies and processes with the goal of reducing the risk of cyber-attacks.

- <u>Internet</u> - A huge, connected network that connects computers all over the world to help people share information, communicate, or game when connected to it.

- <u>WIFI</u> - A way for your computer to connect and talk to other computers using a radio wave without wires connecting the computers.

- <u>IP address</u> - IP stands for Internet Protocol. It is a unique address number used to identify devices on an internet like a postal address, identify home or someone's address.

- <u>Phishing</u> - An attempt to steal other people's personal information, such as passwords, while pretending to come from a legitimate source.

- <u>Two step-verification</u> - A requirement of two steps to access your account. Even though someone finds out what your password is, they still cannot get into your account without entering a second code sent to your email or text.

About The Author

Zinet Kemal, an immigrant from Ethiopia, currently resides in Minnesota. She has been married for over 12 years and is a mother of four children. Zinet earned a Bachelor of Science degree in Computer Science and the Bachelor of Law (LLB). She is currently pursuing her master's degree in Cybersecurity from Georgia Tech University. She works for a Fortune 500 company as an Associate Cloud Security Engineer. Prior to that, she was a Senior Information Security Engineer for the State of Minnesota.

During the pandemic, Zinet noticed how her children were spending more time online gaming or for school. With that exposure she also saw two of her children's gaming accounts hacked on more than two occasions. Their online experiences motivated her to write this story to teach children the important message of online safety.

Being a Black immigrant woman who transitioned into the cybersecurity field, Zinet has learned about the glaring lack of gender and racial diversity within the industry. She hopes to convey a second important message, to spark interest in young readers, especially girls, to consider cybersecurity as an exciting and meaningful career option they can explore.

Zinet is also a #1 Amazon bestseller and award-winning author of the children's book "Proud in Her Hijab."

  @ZinetsBookshelf   www.zinetkemal.com

About The Illustrator

My name is Sasha Izmaylova and I'm an illustrator from Russia. I drew illustrations for the book you hold in your hands. It was an inspiring journey for me, because I had a chance to learn more about Zinet, her family and culture.

I felt like we were on the same page, so I was happy creating beautiful illustrations for the story. I believe that constant learning is key to professional and personal success. That's why my style is changing with my skill. If you want to see how it shifts and to learn more about me, you can visit my Instagram page @sasha_is_may and contact me. I'll be happy to get a few comments about my work!

@sasha_is_may sashaizm96@gmail.com

The Official Coloring Book

Oh, No... Hacked Again!
A Story About Online Safety
Coloring Book

Original Story by: Zinet Kemal

Illustrated by: Sasha Izmaylova

Available On Amazon Now!